Review:

"For a few years, I've wanted to write a novel people would read and go "oooh" and "ahhh." But now, after reading this book, I'd rather drop that and begin making my own personal graphic novel that people could read and relate to for story and art."

Steve Mamay

Horses about Hope:
the art of myth, legend, and graphic writing

Maryann Pasda DiEdwardo and Patricia J. Pasda

Bloomington, IN
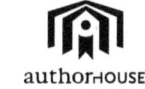
authorHOUSE®
Milton Keynes, UK

AuthorHouse™
1663 Liberty Drive, Suite 200
Bloomington, IN 47403
www.authorhouse.com
Phone: 1-800-839-8640

AuthorHouse™ UK Ltd.
500 Avebury Boulevard
Central Milton Keynes, MK9 2BE
www.authorhouse.co.uk
Phone: 08001974150

This book is a work of non-fiction. Unless otherwise noted, the author and the publisher make no explicit guarantees as to the accuracy of the information contained in this book and in some cases, names of people and places have been altered to protect their privacy.

First published by AuthorHouse 6/4/2007

ISBN: 978-1-4343-0447-6 (sc)

Printed in the United States of America
Bloomington, Indiana

This book is printed on acid-free paper.

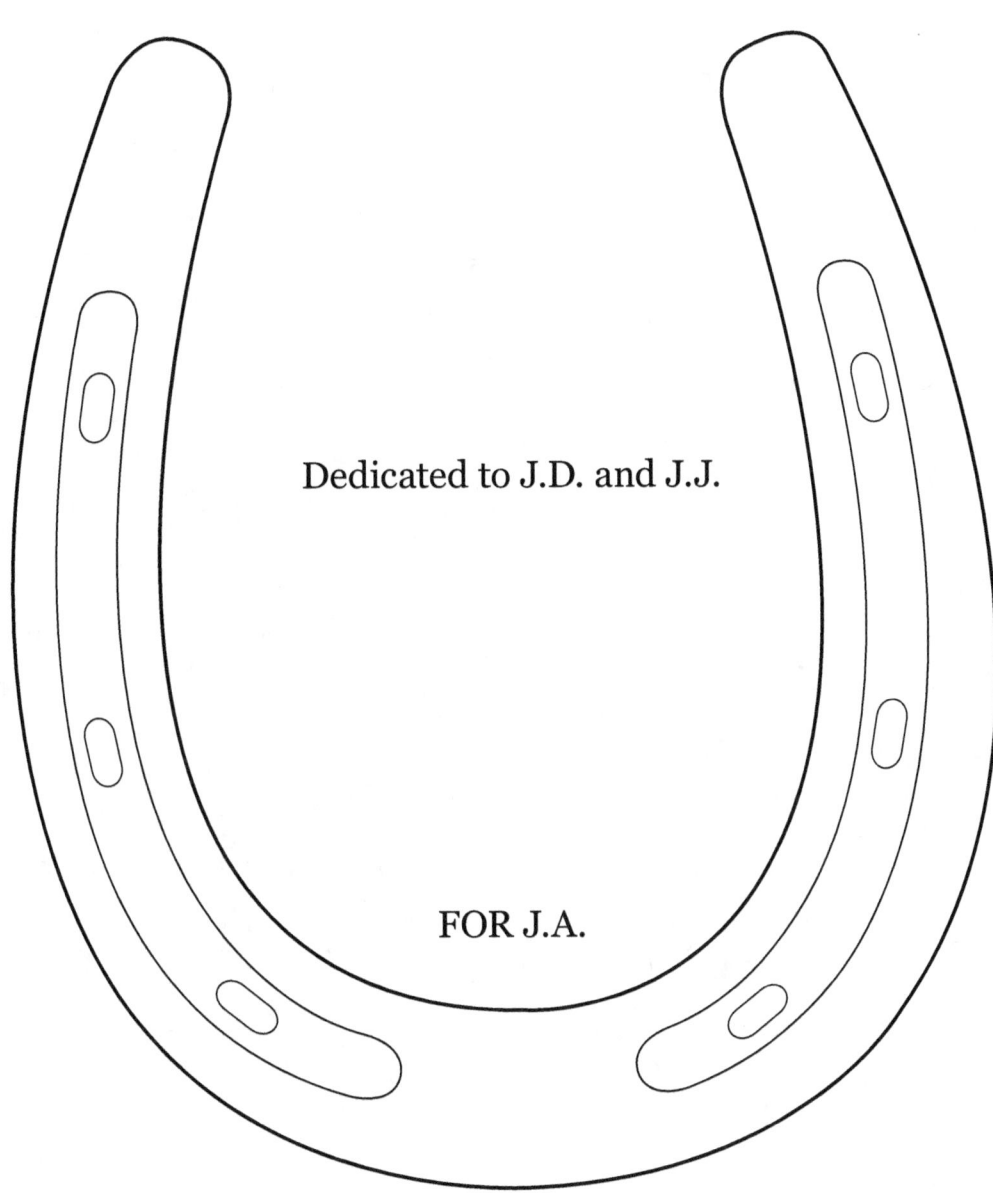

Dedicated to J.D. and J.J.

FOR J.A.

Contents

"For a few years, I've wanted to write a novel people would read and go 'oooh' and 'ahhh'. But now, after reading this book, I'd rather drop that and begin making my own personal graphic novel that people could read and relate to for story and art."

Steve Mamay

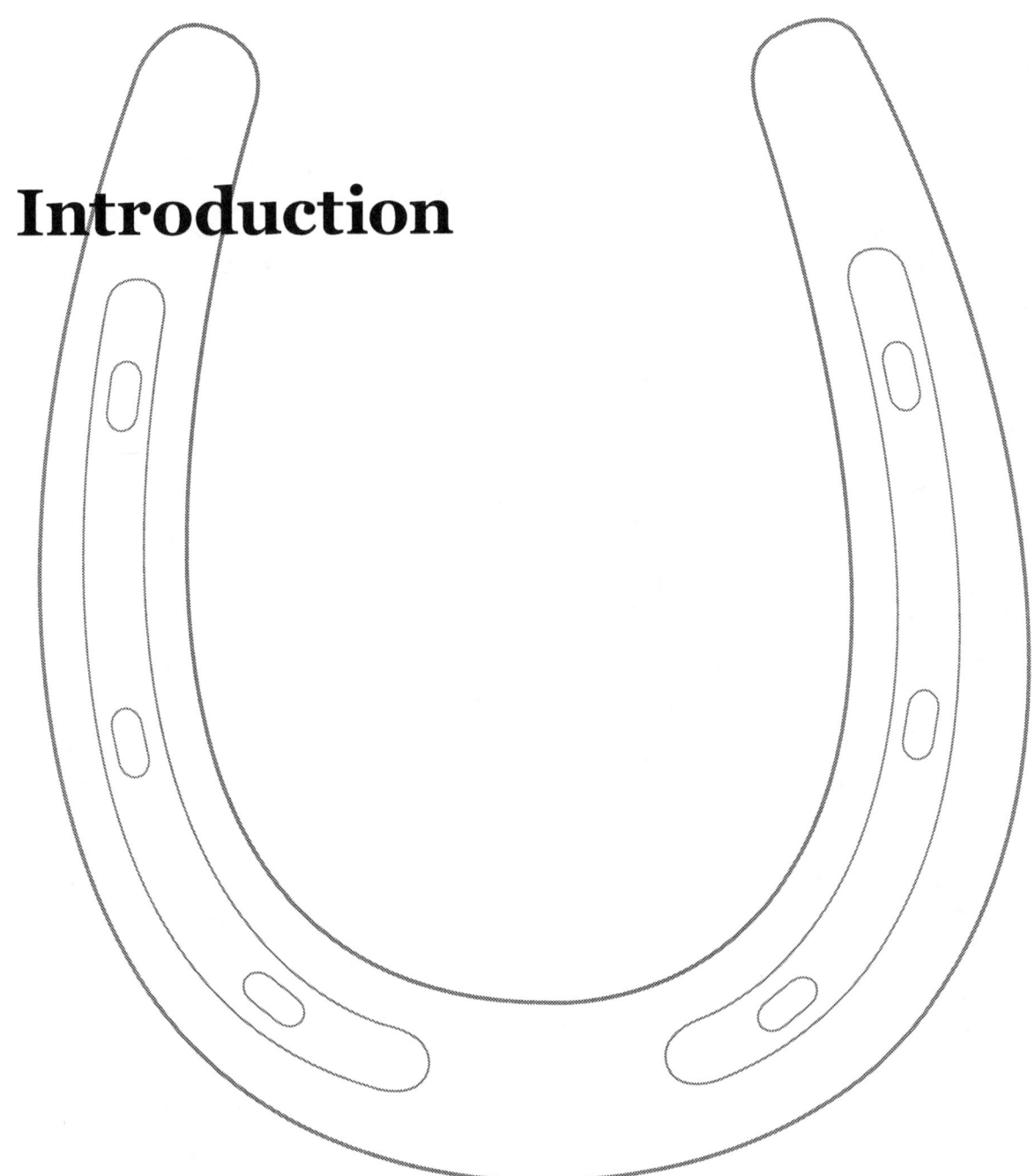

Introduction

Our art work is blended with words that speak to our readers and art novel in graphic design pages to add visual voice. The characters of the tale are the mythological representations of thought in line form. Visual representation stimulates the mind to create pictures as the reader becomes artist within the text. Principal design attributes of our graphic writing text produce a story, a method of teaching, a paradigm for education via graphic writing as a new genre.

We utilize myth as literature. We find that the quest myth translates to the definition of the quest of the artist within the reality of the creative process.

GRAPHIC WRITING teaches the principles of form as story, line as a writing tool, and life story as primary function of the graphic writer. The definite and the indefinite become combined to create story based upon legend within the writer and the topic as well as myth as theoretical basis for writing and creative thought. The human community defines order with friendship and love as the story represents the reader's dreams of perfect life dream.

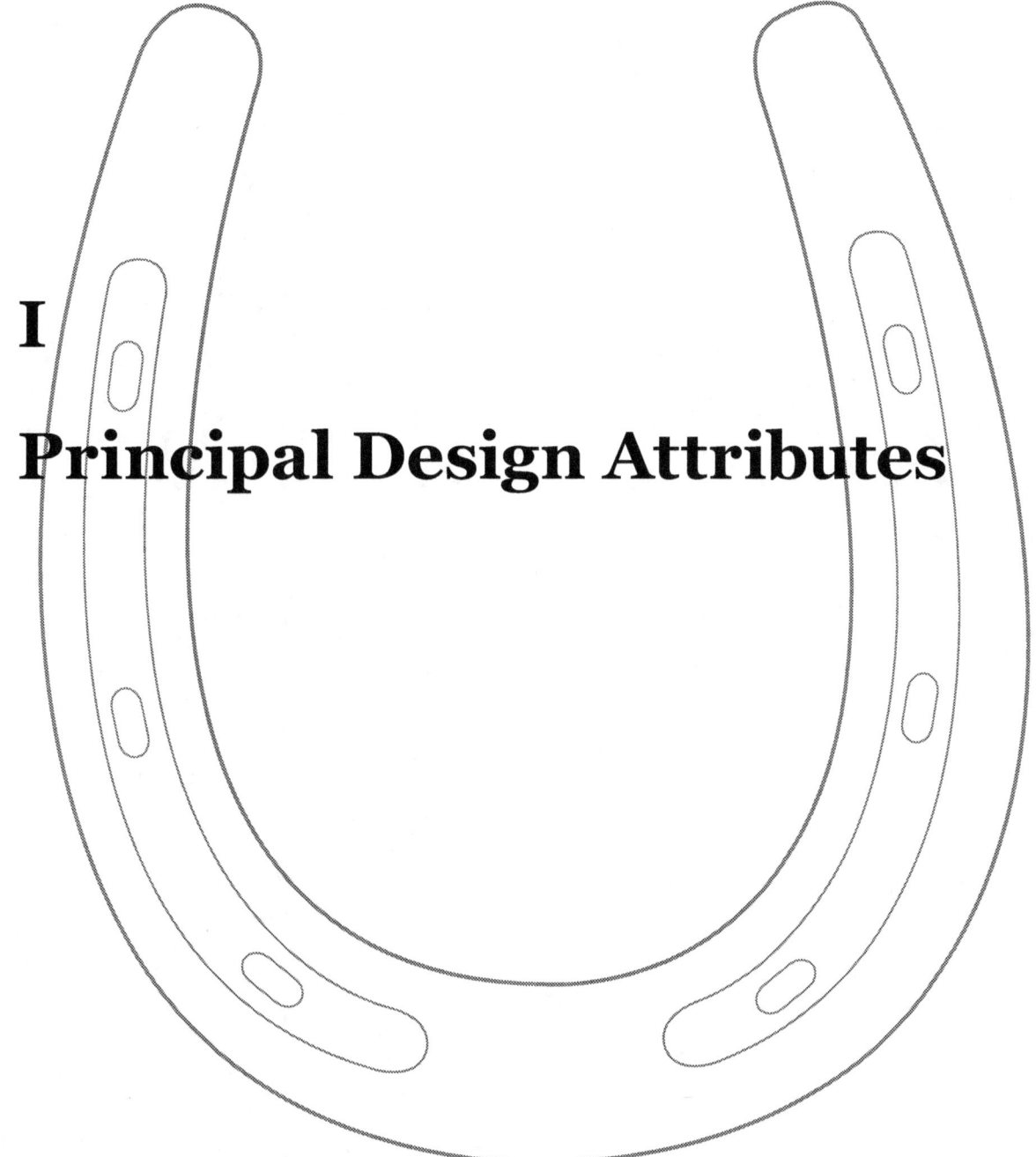

I
Principal Design Attributes

The artist creates a novella or short novel in the form of a series of artful representations with line as the functioning method of creativity. The result is a graphic writing project that is filled with emotion, plot, character, theme, style and tone. Mood is set up by the natural process of graphic writing that focuses the mind of the reader on two elements: art and writing. Together, the two create a blending of activity that reach into the mind and stimulate the creative process.

Story becomes the mode of the mind and art becomes the language. The use of graphic writing within our educational system may change the ability of students to achieve since an early development of the artistic creative process may allow students to invent and voice their imaginings.

From the early beginnings of time, the human has created form as a function of the human capacity to reach out and form therefore is a language. Paradoxically, graphic form then becomes a language. We promote graphic art novella as a form to speak to others in a visual language with hand written text by the artist to add language to art.

The graphic writing project instills a visual memory seed that grows inside the mind and nourishes the instincts of artistic temperament. Joy within the artistic endeavor becomes a visual experience where the writer or graphic writer can tell a story through pictures that has been the cornerstone of the human creative mind.

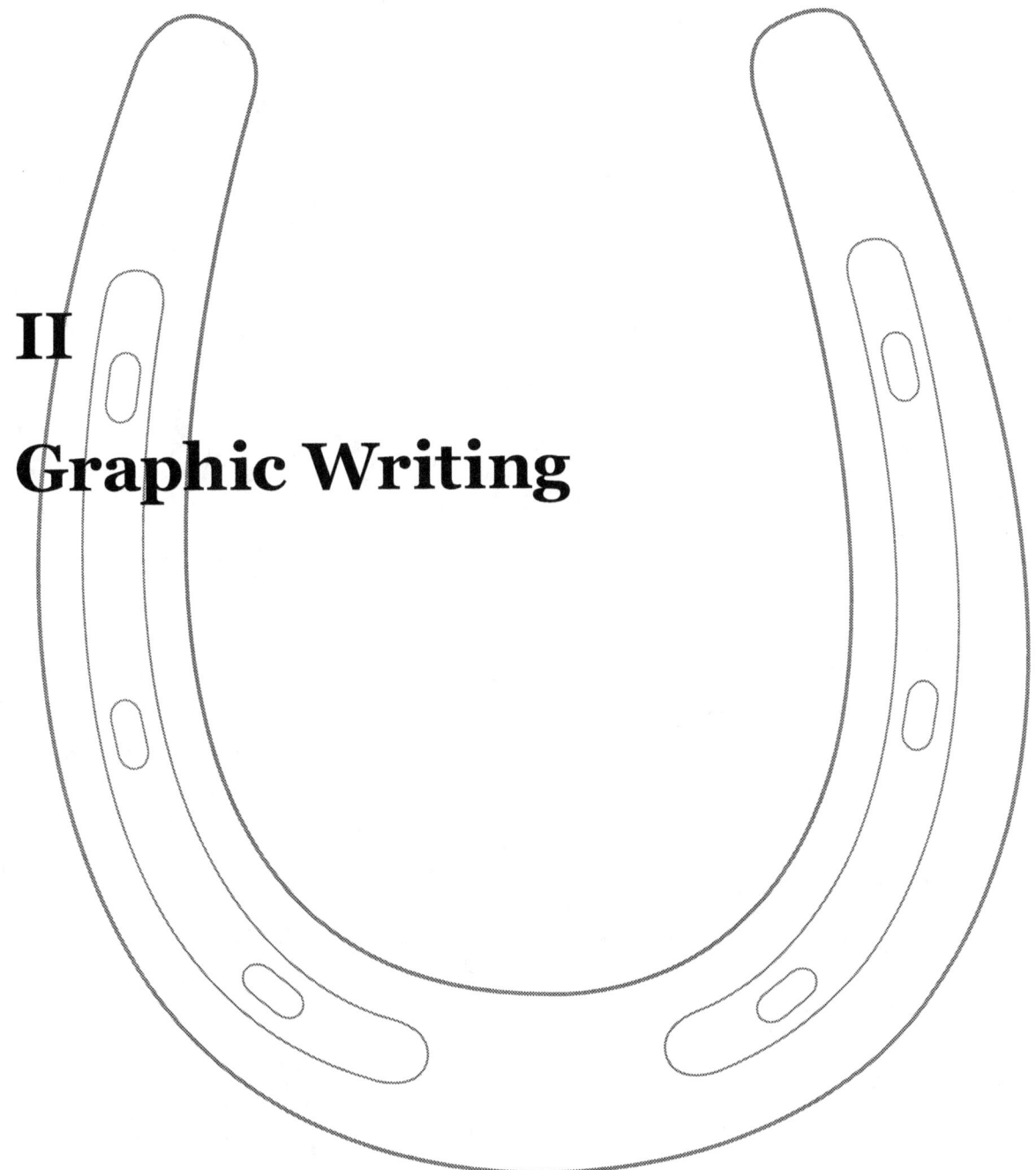

II
Graphic Writing

Art and the Growing Child has been our focus as scholars for we open the doors to fine art as a doorway or path to myth, legend and graphic writing for all ages to grow as thinkers and doers.

Myth lends the artist as a form of story to develop value curtains or layers of foreground to the farthest point in the graphic written design. Use ballpoint pen, pencil, watercolor or other mediums to build the story as you feel the characters.

Legend takes over as the story progresses through a series of ups and downs to develop plot as graphic writers think in terms of art. Furthermore, create as many layers as you need to show the story. But wait for the graphic art to set up the legend and view the art as paramount to the production of the piece.

Our graphic novel interprets story through the art of drawing.

At this point in our study of fine art as a path to self knowledge and creative way of perception, we seek to design educational projects to provide artistic development for K-adult educational program development, seminar development, coordinated programs for educational institutions for a synthesis of fine arts in educational institutions with virtual classroom development to promote art and the growing child.

Therefore, our work represents the vision of the artful way of training a human child to grow.

Pedagogy of our graphic world begins with sketches that are based upon myth. The meaning of a myth resounds with fairy tale base upon life as beautiful and finesse with moral subjects and biblical or spiritual themes. Add the final message with legend of story that you know from memory or other sources. Exaggerate the graphic writing with strong values or vibrant dark and light. Finish with mood by allowing the tones to tell the story.

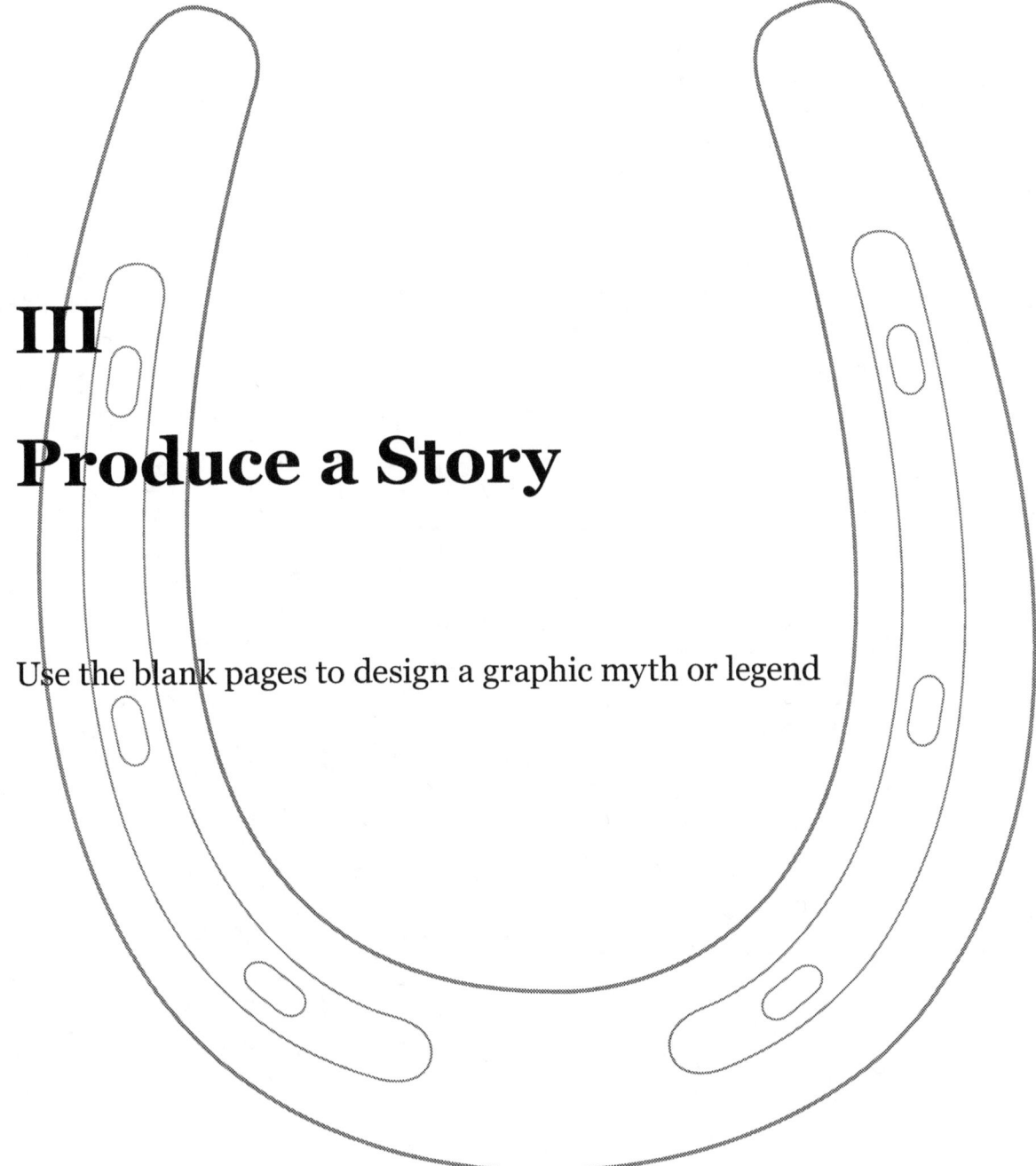

III

Produce a Story

Use the blank pages to design a graphic myth or legend

Writing has a new meaning in the graphic setting

We are making our own history; we use our own responses and we see language as metaphor.

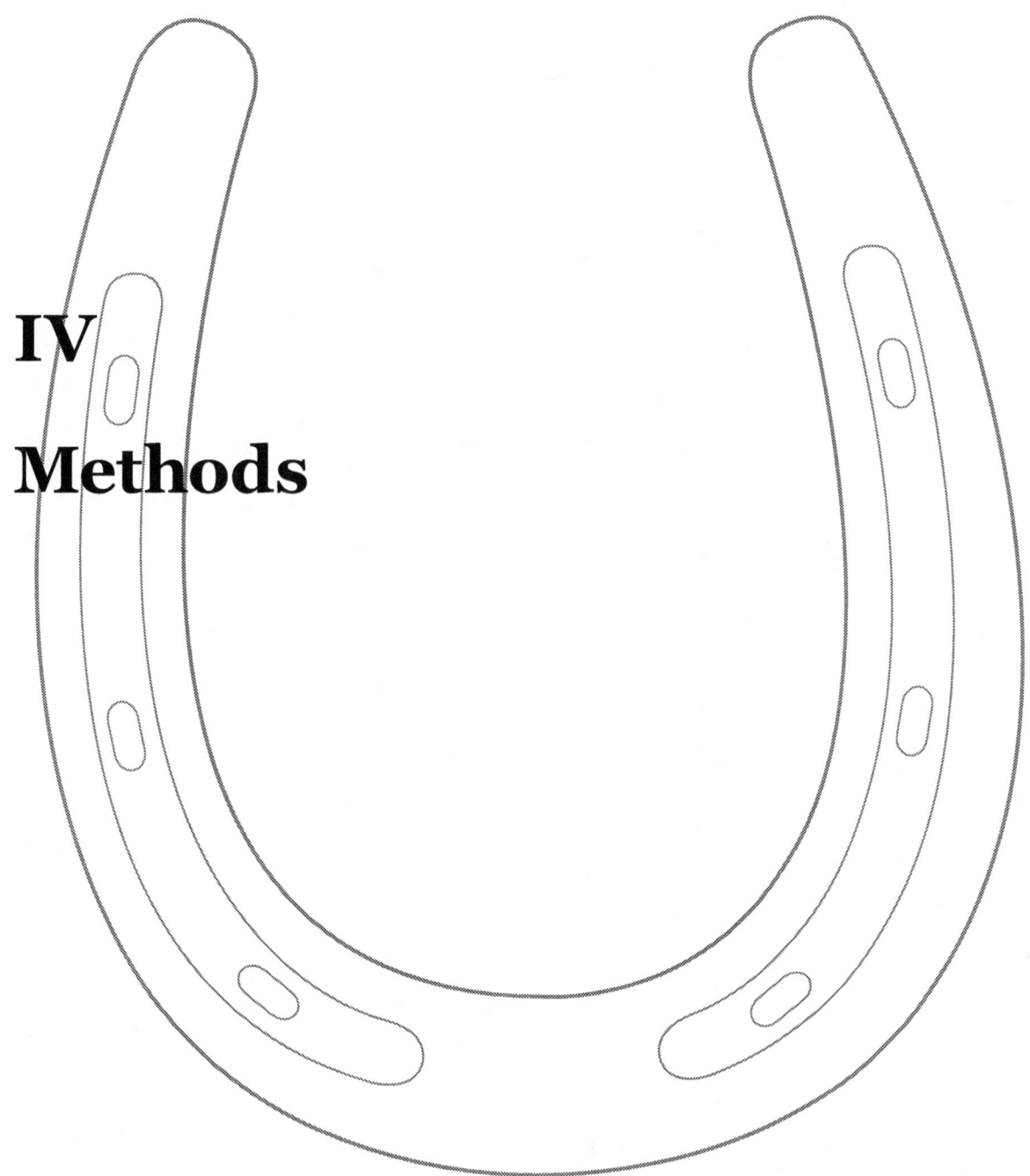

IV
Methods

Graphic art is musical. Variation is a compositional technique borrowed from music which aims at creating artistic order through the exploitation and development of a theme or motif. Variations became a preferred form of a musical composition at the beginning of the 18th century. They were later taken up by Beethoven who added the possibility of transforming the themes and can also be used in philosophy and the arts. Literature, especially the 20th century novel, uses variations by treating them as differentia work in our text for example or another work submitted to various modes of illumination. The whole set of variations found within a work defines the identity of the chosen theme.

glossary of graphic art terms

aim - the intention of the author of a literary work

analysis - the separation of the whole to study the parts - the author's thesis - the structure of the text

anecdote - a short narrative of an interesting, amusing, or biographical incident

appeal - the ability of an author to attract the reader

archetype - a typical or recurring theme, image, character, narrative design, or other literary phenomenon that has been in literature from the beginning and regularly appears - archetypes provide a basis for connecting one work to another and enable the reader to integrate and unify the literary experience.

canon - when applied to an individual author, the sum total of works verifiably written by that author - generally means range of works that a consensus of scholars consider great

climax - the turning point, the third part of plot structure, the point when the action stops rising and begins reversing

connotation - what is suggested by a word, apart from what it explicitly describes contemplative rumination - a term used in contemporary criticism - to ponder or think again about an idea

materials – pen an dink, pencil, ink and brush offer the graphic writer the tools to design pages of text and graphic art to tell the myth or legend

natural world components – the diversity of mountains, forests, plains, marshes, and water offer an abundance of materials

paradox - a self-contradictory or nonsensical proposition that proves to be well founded or partially true

parody - adaptation of preceding styles

plot – the story line

setting – place for the artist to set the tale

syntax - the way words are put together to form phrases, clauses, and sentences

Projects

U Graphic design can be a pattern like a short story. Pick a literary work and create graphic written design. Seek to pay copyright payment if the work was published after 1923.

"The Story of an Hour"

or a play <u>Hamlet</u>

"I Stand Here Ironing"
    by Tillie Olson

"Fiesta 1980"
    by Junot Diaz

"Sonny's Blues"
    by James Baldwin

"This is What It Means To Say Phoenix, Arizona"
    by Sherman Alexie

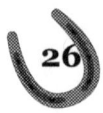

"Scar"

    by Amy Tan.

"Yellow Woman"

    by Leslie Marmon Silko

"Professions for Women"

    by Virginia Woolf

"Lady Lapdog"

    by Anton Chekhov

"Death of a Son"

    by Njabulo S. Nbebele

"Hills Like White Elephants"

    by Ernest Hemingway

"Eveline"

    by James Joyce

"Shiloh"

    by Bobbie Ann Mason

"The Yellow Wallpaper"

by Charlotte Perkins Gilman

"Tickets, Please"

by D.H. Lawrence

"My Life with the Wave"

by Octavio Paz

"The Chase"

by Alberto Moravia

"The Jilting of Granny Weatherall"

by Katherine Anne Porter.

"I'm Your Horse in the Night"

by Luisa Valenzuela

"American Ignorance of War"

by Czeslaw Milosz

"War"

by Luigi Pirandello

"The Shawl"

    by Cynthia Ozick

"The War Generation"

    by Shusaku Endo

"The Things They Carried"

    by Tim O'Brien

"Ralph the Duck"

    by Frederick Busch.

"Amnesty"

    by Nadine Gordimer

"Harrison Bergeron"

    by Kurt Vonnegut

"Girls at War"

    by Chinua Achebe

"The Handsomest Drowned Man in the World"

    by Gabriel Garcia Marquez

"The Third and Fina Continent"

    by Jhumpa Lahiri

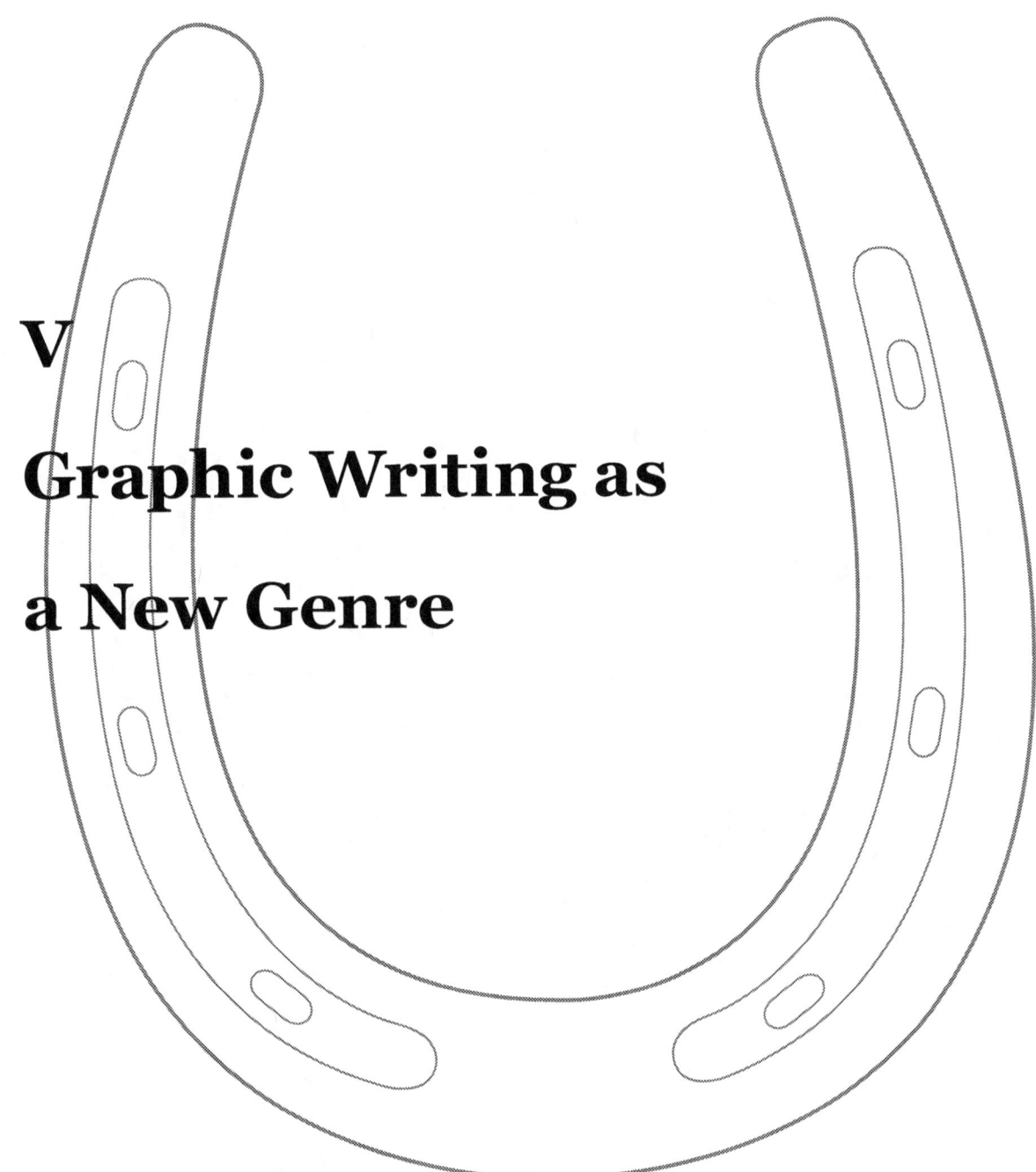

V

Graphic Writing as

a New Genre

Students who read daily succeed. Your book is your life experience. Get to know the books required and use them daily as a part of life. Read the works and pick your favorite writers to use for research projects. Ask if you can write on writers who are not represented in the required texts.

Use every activity that you come across in the class experience including telephone or real face to face conferences, chat experiences, group talks, coffeehouse days, presentations of others or web searches. ALL these activities are the stuff of writing as we write about our lives. For instance, a paper may be a review of a coffeehouse day and an analysis of student presentations.

Write about the lectures, web experiences like video streaming searches and reviews, group research library searches, movies you see on weekends, theatre, field trips to art museums or to your relative's home, library lessons online or in the library, group experiences, class happenings, chats, or write poetry fiction drama within the essay or author personality integration such as a letter to your author or a letter to your friend. Live your writing and you will succeed.

Write a play graphically with your group or write a newspaper article to publish in a class newsletter or a class website. Develop a class website or a class power point series.

After all, you are the writer now and you are making history.

Technology and Graphic Writing are Compatible

Chats can be coffeehouse days where you write about your experiences in writing and share thoughts on your own life as writing topics or to add to writing topics. I save blackboard chats; they are documents you can refer to as citations or you can use as preliminary parts of papers. Chats can be poetry fiction drama presentations where students post a short set of web sites or literary terms or parts of writing and gain discussion journal points or use the experience actually to write a paper. Papers can be ABOUT chats. Live internet experiences are life and we write about life or about others who understand aspects of the human condition. Blogs are live writing process as well. Create a group blog and use that for a presentation or a team paper.

Graphic Writing

The following curriculum designs are suitable for K-adult classes in traditional and virtual settings.

Graphic Writing Contextual Framework

1. Define Purpose of Lesson

2. Identify Transformational Qualities

3. List Transformational Goals

4. Art Selection or Selections

5. Literary Work or Works

6. Contextual Patterns of Art and Literature

7. Annotation of Art Works and Literary Work or Works

8. Metaphors in Context of Art and Literary Works

9. Compare and Contrast Art and Literature

10. Context and Art Applied to Research

11. Types of Prose

   To Narrate

   To Explain

   To Describe

   To Define

   To Compare and Contrast

   To Analyze

   To Argue

12. Journal Discussions

13. Technology Interactions

14. Group

   Discussions

   Peer Critique

   Project

15. Writing Process

    Brainstorming

    Clustering

    THESIS STATEMENT

    Outlining

    Drafting

16. CULTURE Student Gains Self Knowledge Evolution of Transformation

17. PRESENT Portfolio

Challenges in Learning Respond to Art as Transformative

U We create independent knowledge seekers through heuristics that we pass on in the distance learning setting. Applicable use of information requires that we see knowledge acquisition as amorphous and changing. We infuse cognitive abilities of our students by helping them "think" as one of my students suggested. Students progress as creative thinkers and graphic designers within ANY major study area.

With the graphic design educational framework, the course enlightens their linguistic intelligence through analysis of literature, logical-mathematical intelligence through electronic activities, their musical intelligence, their spatial intelligence as they can create their own learning space to work in the virtual setting without classroom anxiety, their bodily kinesthetic intelligence since they can move about when they need to in the atmosphere of virtual learning, their naturalistic intelligence when they can pet the cat or tend the plants as they write a paper, their personal intelligences through virtual discussions, and their existential intelligence if applicable to writing in activities such as Biblical allusions or the nature of spiritual in literature.

Curriculum Design #1

Paper 1 500 words with three pages of art based graphic representations

Paper 2 500 words with three pages of art based graphic representations

Paper 3 500 words with three pages of art based graphic representations

Paper 4 1500 words with ten pages of art based graphic representations

Curriculum Design #2

Paper 1 500 words with three pages of art based graphic representations

Paper 2 500 words with three pages of art based graphic representations

Paper 4 2000 words with twenty pages of art based graphic representations

Curriculum Design #3

Paper 1 1500 words with three pages of art based graphic representations

Paper 4 1500 words with twenty-five pages of art based graphic representations

Curriculum Design #4

Paper 4 3000 words with thirty pages of art based graphic representations

Curriculum Design #5

Paper 4 2500 words with forty pages of art based graphic representations completed technology project of audio, video, power point or other technology project to feature paper thesis resources planning and implementation

Curriculum Design #6

Student writes all papers with one team of two or more students.

Team Paper 1 1000 words with three pages of art based graphic representations

Team Paper 4 1500 words with twenty pages of art based graphic representations

Technology projects in team effort to supplement papers

Curriculum Design #7

Student writes one paper with one team of two or more students.

Paper 1 1000 words with three pages of art based graphic representations

Team Paper 4 1500 words with thirty pages of art based graphic representations

Technology project with team

Read required literary and graphic artists works and establish means of understanding historical background, author and artist biographies, and alternative means of creativity of the work such as film or documentary on the writer. Film is a powerful tool in the understanding of literature. Students create their own primary sources such as interviews, reader's theatre on a chat type of group setting where we act out a virtual scene from a play as part of a team effort and experience to write about, a fiction or poetic work create by class members as an original primary document.

The following list presents discussion teams and group collaborative efforts:

1. Creating a class glossary of graphic writing terms that apply to literature

2. Creating a class list of quotations from famous artists in a group of one or more

3. Creating links to web sites on graphic writing as a viable art form

4. Haiku Book based on reader's graphic interpretations

5. Graphic Art as Theatre

6. Interview with family or co-worker about reaction to art

7. Designing a website

8. Designing a power point

9. Creating a document that can be shared with others in a small group

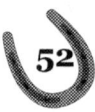
Graphic art can be based on music lyrics as literature, film comparison to analyze literature, and technology as literary study (power point, comparison of web sites, combination of technology like chat programs and newsletters, may help student succeed in literature based technology emphasized curriculums.

Variation is a compositional technique borrowed from music which aims at creating artistic order through the exploitation and development of a theme or motif. Variations became a preferred form of a musical composition at the beginning of the 18th century. They were later taken up by Beethoven who added the possibility of transforming the themes and can also be used in philosophy and the arts. Literature, especially the 20th century novel, uses variations by treating them as differentia work in our text for example or another work selected by a student is submitted to various modes of illumination. The whole set of variations found within a work defines the identity of the chosen theme.

Add details to graphic designs by forming pictures in your mind through reference to the voices of the

DIN Phenomenon

"The phenomenon of the 'Din' or spontaneous playback, may possibly be a sign of language acquisition and music may be a significant factor in activating the 'Din' (Iudin-Nelson, 1997)." Spontaneous playback or the "Din" phenomenon (Iudin-Nelson, 1997) was first noted by Krashen (1983) and refers to the involuntary or spontaneous rehearsal in one's mind of words. The "Din" contributes to the effectiveness of the use of song to engage the students' minds and prepare them to read and write about literature. Repetition of language and literary skills can be taught through the use of song lyrics and the knowledge that the students repeat patterns of favorite songs in their heads. The brain function then reinforces the ability to think about literature in the same or similar way. Understanding song lyrics as poetry aids the understanding of language.

More Projects

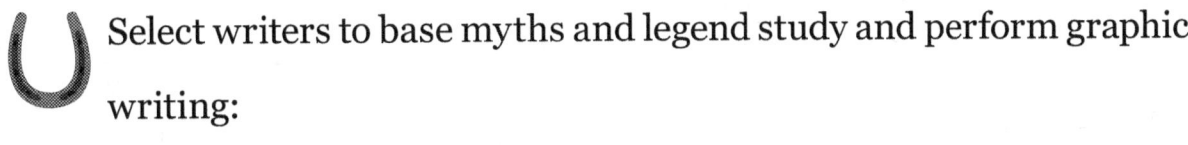 Select writers to base myths and legend study and perform graphic writing:

Ben Johnson

Amiri Baraka

W.D. Snodgrass

Martin Espada

Sylvia Plath

Simon Ortiz

Li-Young Lee

Seamus Heaney

Audre Lorde

Lyn Lifshin

Jamaica Kincaid

Anne Sexton

Pat Mora

Maxine Kumin

Margaret Walker

Etheridge Knight

Lord Randal

Anne Bradstreet

William Wordsworth

Frances Ellen Watkins Harper

D. H. Lawrence

Harold A. Zlotnik

W.H. Auden

Lao-tzu

Wilfred Owen

Mary Jo Salter

Langston Hughes

Gwendolyn Brooks

Etheridge Knight

Allen Ginsberg

Gloria Anzaldua

Joy Harjo

Susan Griffin

Maya Angelou

Wole Soyinka

Carolyn Forche

Charlotte Delbo

Jonathan Swift

William Blake

Thomas Hardy

Paul Laurence Dunbar

Hart Crane

Anna Deavere Smith

Lorraine Hansberry

William Shakespeare

John Donne

Andrew Marvell

Matthew Arnold

William Blake

Pablo Neruda

Leopold-Sedar Senghor

Gary Synder

Liz Rosenberg

Huda Naamani

Marge Piercy

Cherrie Moraga

Anne Sexton

Anna Akhmatova

T.S. Eliot

Robert Herrick

Lord Byron

John Keats

Elizabeth Barrett Browning

Edgar Arlington Robinson

Edna St. Vincent Millay

E..E. Cummings

Adrienne Rich

Yeats

Judith Emlyn Johnson

Tagore

Rainer Maria Rilke

Wordsworth

Coleridge

Poe

Whitman

Dickinson

Yeats

Roethke

Dylan Thomas

James Wright

Wallace Stevens

Cathy Song

References

DiEdwardo, Mary Ann. (2004). "Music Transforms the College English Classroom." Diss. California Coast University, Santa Ana, California.

Iudin-Nelson, Laurie June. (1997). "Songs in the L2 Syllabus Integrating the Study of Russian Language and Culture." Diss. U of Wisconsin, Madison.

Krashen, Stephen D. (1989). *Language Acquisition and Language Education. 2nd ed.* Language Teaching Methodology. New York: Prentice.

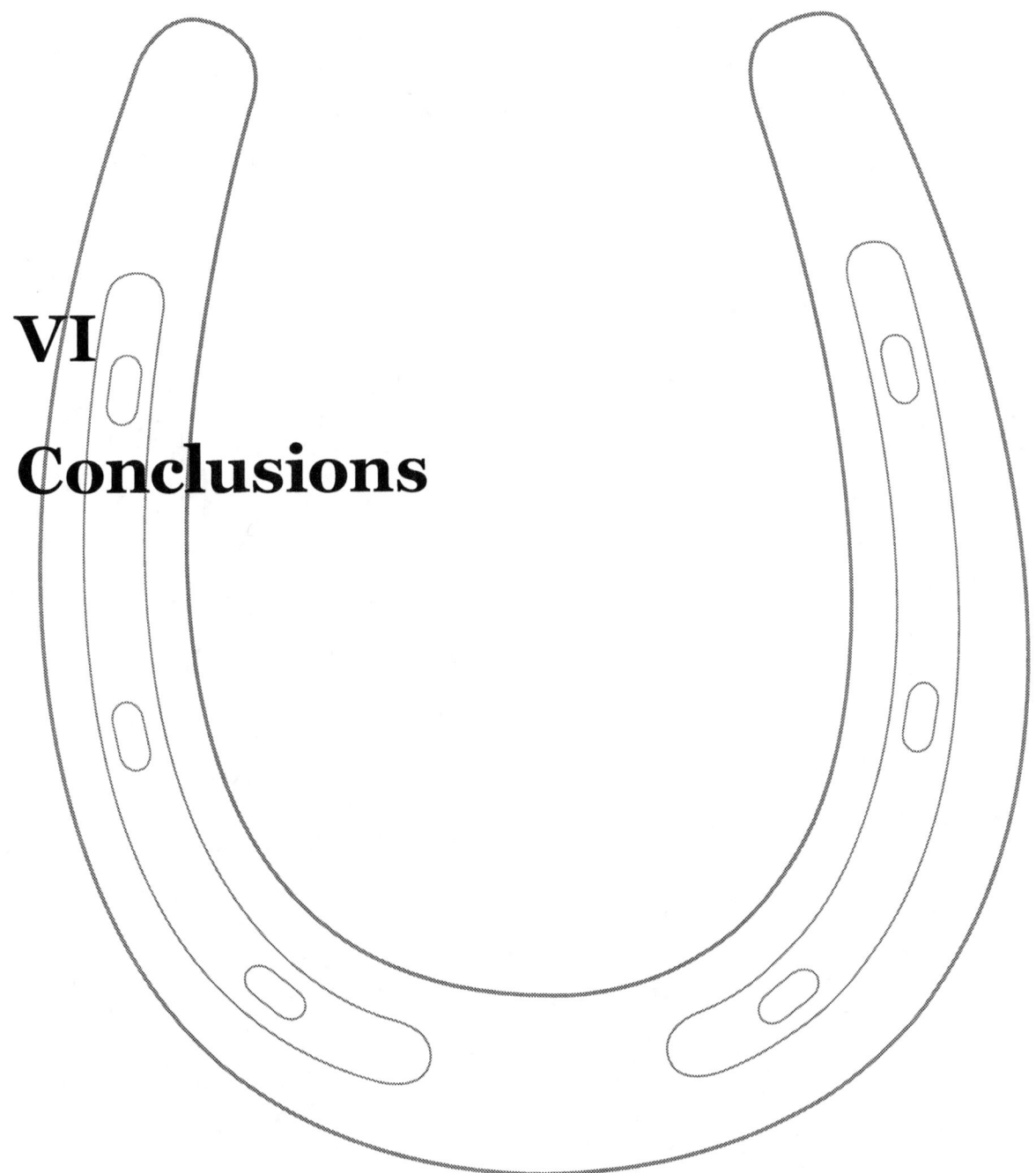

VI
Conclusions

Graphic writing, new classification, combines the artistic visual talent with the inner writing talent to envelop the creator and soar into a new genre or method of design. Therefore, the vast majority of the graphic writing arena is new. The human mind varies in capacity to read and observe as time befits us to create new ways of visualization and creation. Why not combine art with writing to design? The young can add scribbles to writing projects to expand thoughts and story as life story becomes paramount to thinking.

ESSAY

Designing Curriculums for Students with Disabilities through Fine Art as a Doorway to Learning

A study of past heroes such as Katharine Hepburn leads educators to design new curriculum strategies for educational paradigms. Hepburn's legacy, a devotion to theatre art as a way of life, is a captivating and transcending vision for our students in the virtual setting. Multi arts educational frameworks enhance virtual platforms and focus the student on the use of the past to create a new history or new reader response in literature computer based virtual classes.

Write about the myth you feel every day as you explore different types of literature, experiences like video streaming searches and reviews, group research library searches, movies you see on weekends, theatre, field trips to art museums or to your relative's home, library visits, group experiences, happenings, chats, or write poetry fiction drama within the essay or author personality integration such as a letter to your author or a letter to your friend about your graphic writing study.

. . . .

Writers select a certain syntax to represent voice. Syntax is word order, an excellent paper topic and/or thesis with focus on analysis of writing craft and voice of both student writer and primary and secondary source writers. I encouraged writers and artists to use electronic portfolio which means that students perform writing assignments through the virtual means. Essentially, we are developing writing ability through finding personal writer voice meaning artist's styles, contents, and formats.

For the most part, in graphic writing, diction forms voice. Diction is word choice. Writers may use the lyrics of songs to study the use of diction. The word choice of a song writer resembles the word choice of an essayist or prose writer. We use thesis (or chorus) to unify the piece through language. Find your voice in my class through the use of catalysts such as music or film or critical analysis. Music in the virtual language alternative setting improves students' reading and writing skills. Add details by reference to the voices of the writers of your chosen library resources for your Works Cited and alluding to our text book readings.

Voice creates thesis. Use third person with a combination of elements to write a strong argumentative position based thesis: three elements of language such as diction, voice, syntax, paired with an active verb to show analysis, an element of literary skill such as fiction, drama, poetry, and add a primary source or author. For instance, Shakespeare utilizes voice, diction and syntax in the monologues of <u>Hamlet</u> to create characterization.

After all, you are the writer now and you are making history.

In my teaching strategies, I use a process of understanding cognitive function called Multiple Intelligences. Based on Howard Gardner's Theory, my work includes applications of Gardner's definition of intelligence as a "biopsychological potential" (Gardner, 2004, page 29) of intelligences, in effect a critique of intelligence as a single entity which is not movable or changeable. I am integrating the newest technology into my distance classes such as electronic portfolio, blogs, wikis, processfolio (Gardner) web site evaluation and design, paperless class option chat reader's theatre, team newsletters, team papers, framework applied to virtual processfolio, hyperlinks for lectures.

The purpose of my 2003 study was to investigate the significant sustained performance of Northampton Community College students. Five different studies were generated during the period from January 2003 to December 2003. Dependent variables were participants' grades, attendance, writing process, sentence structure, vocabulary, theses statements, paragraphing, reading comprehension, cut and paste method, word processing, drafting, and research paper writing. The researcher used single group post test only to study relationships of dependent variables to the use of modern songs with lyrics and their pedagogical application in the college English classroom at the Northampton Community College. Systematic replication was implemented. This low-constraint research case study attempted to demonstrate a new framework for teaching college English and used a combination of naturalistic observation and classification of variables. The independent variable was curriculum design entitled *Musicality Contextual Framework*. The researcher attempted to find out if the new framework could be carried out.

The subjects in the present study were 70 students in two different sections of English I and three different sections of English II classes.

The May 7th, 2003 Field Test, approved by the Dean of the Northampton Community College Department of Arts and Sciences, officially started the case study research process. The revised Field Test became the actual Survey and was used to question the students in Northampton Community College summer English I as well as fall semester English I and English II 2003 classes.

Results of the analyses of the cross-sectional design were significant, suggesting that comparisons between the use of music in the classroom and the dependent variables may transform, and a correlation exists between music and English I and II. Furthermore, the results suggest that the participation in the listening of music and the selection of favorite music by the student prepare the student to learn about literature, writing, and computer skills appropriate for writing. In particular, grade and thesis writing skill were improved.

References

Dissertation (Pennsylvania State University, Harvard University, Montgomery Community College, Lehigh Carbon Community College, Northampton Community College, DeSales University, Lehigh University, California Coast University own manuscript hard copies)

DiEdwardo, MaryAnn Pasda. <u>Music Transforms the College English Classroom: A Case Study.</u> Dissertation. California Coast University, Santa Ana, CA, 2004.

Gardner, H. (2004) *Changing minds: The art and science of changing our own and other people's minds.* Boston: Harvard Business School Press. Translated into French, Spanish, Japanese, Italian, Korean, Dutch, Portuguese, Greek, Polish, Russian, Turkish, Chinese, Danish; Awarded Strategy + Business's Best Business Books of the Year (2004).

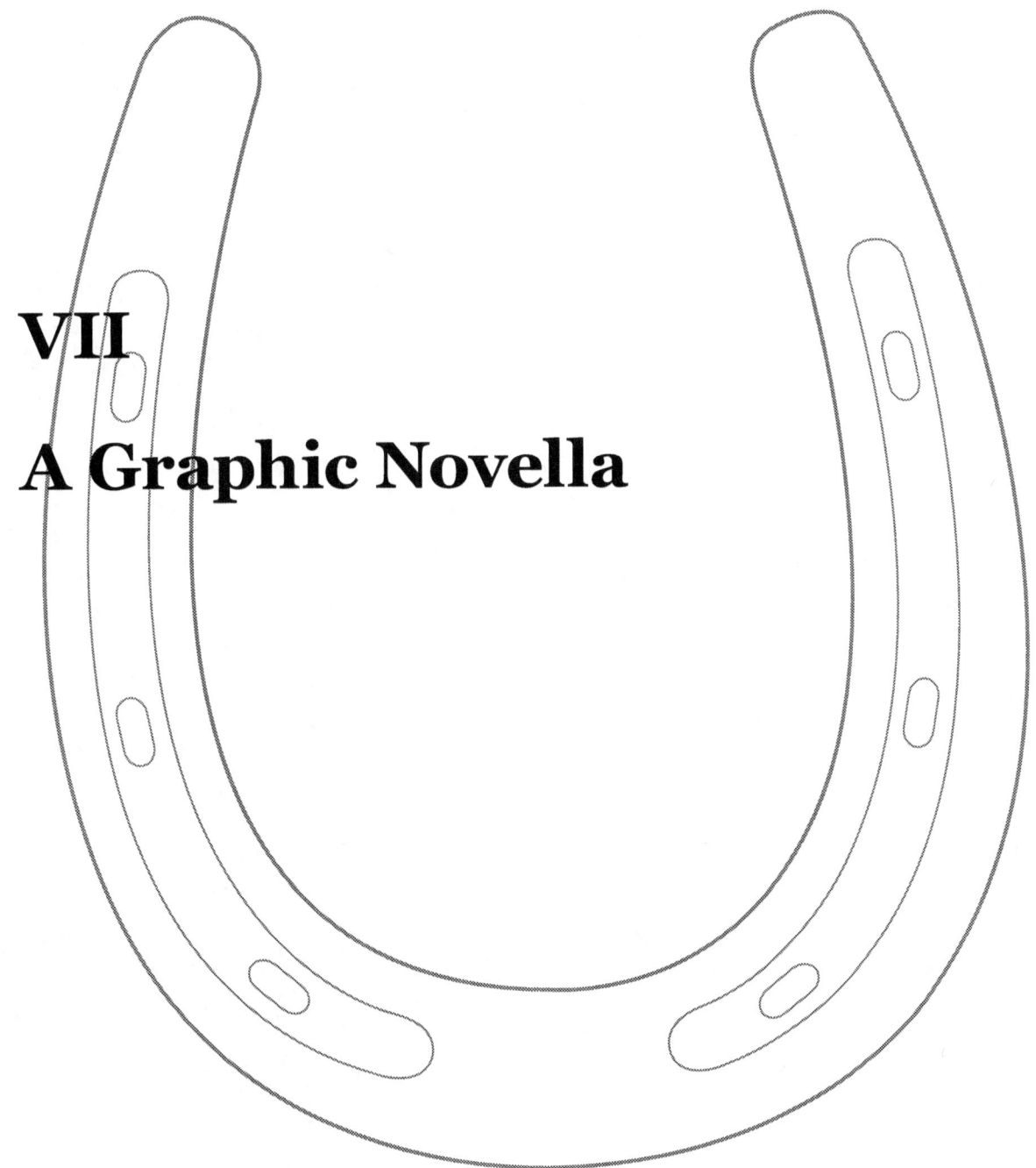

VII
A Graphic Novella

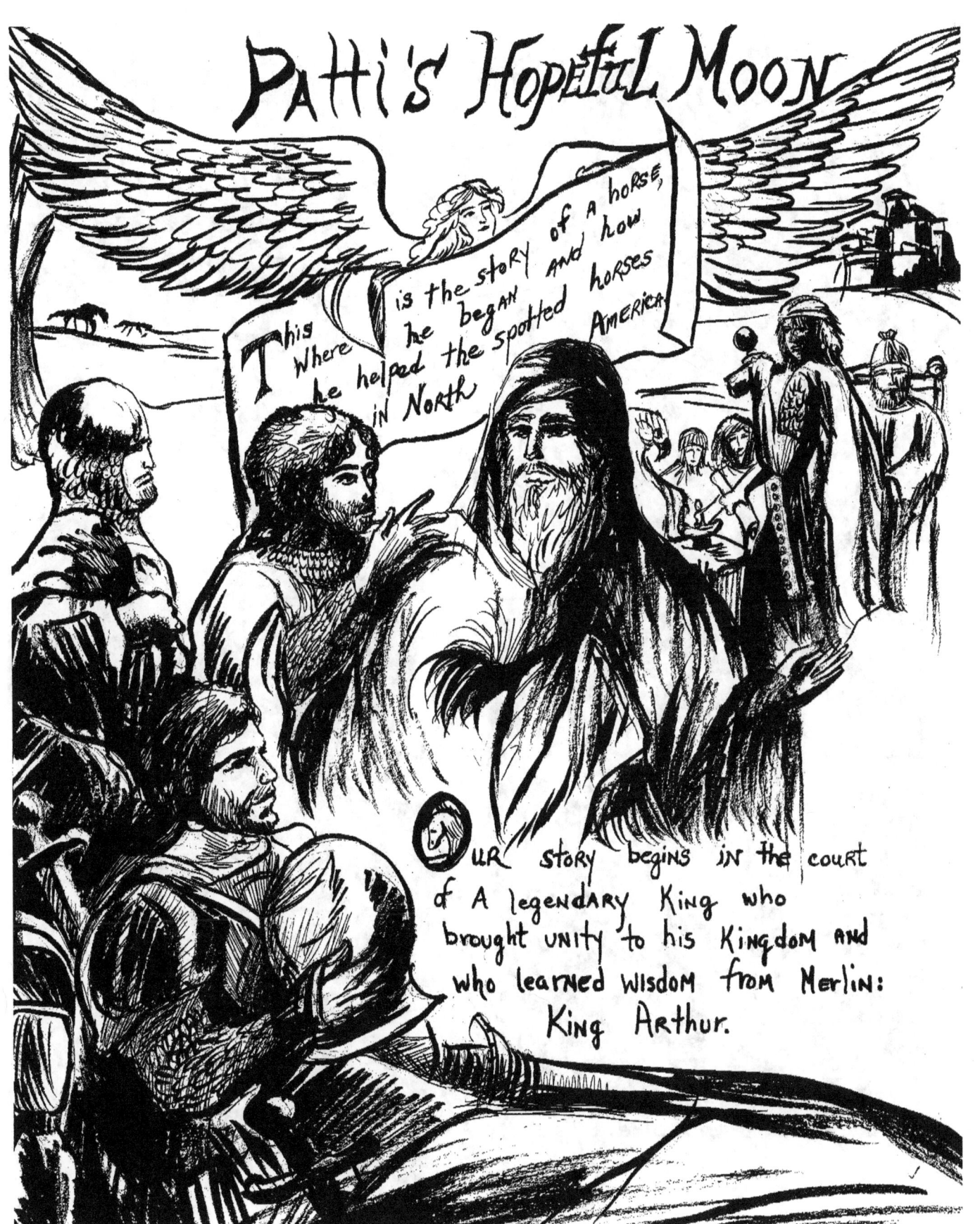

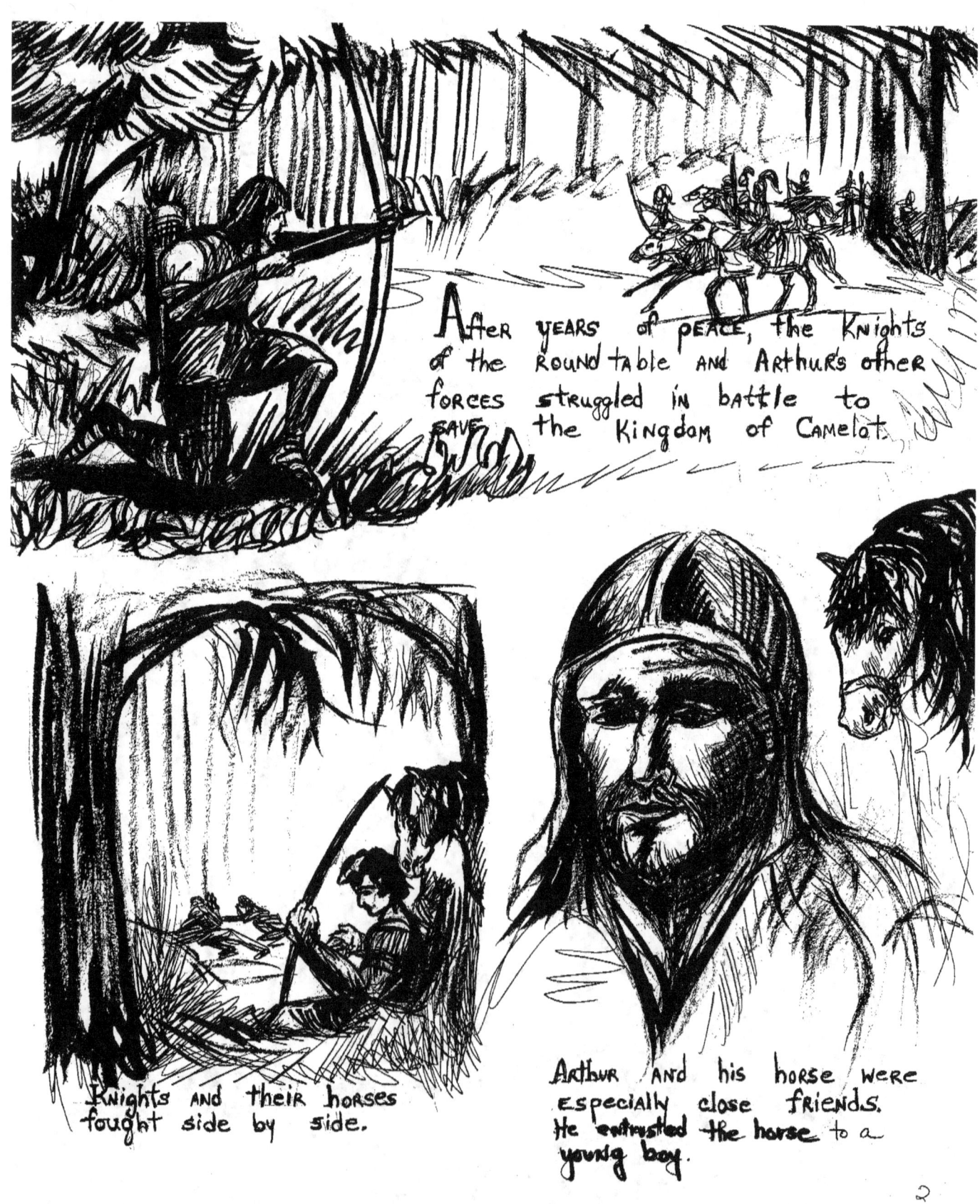

After years of peace, the Knights of the Round Table and Arthur's other forces struggled in battle to save the Kingdom of Camelot.

Knights and their horses fought side by side.

Arthur and his horse were especially close friends. He entrusted the horse to a young boy.

2

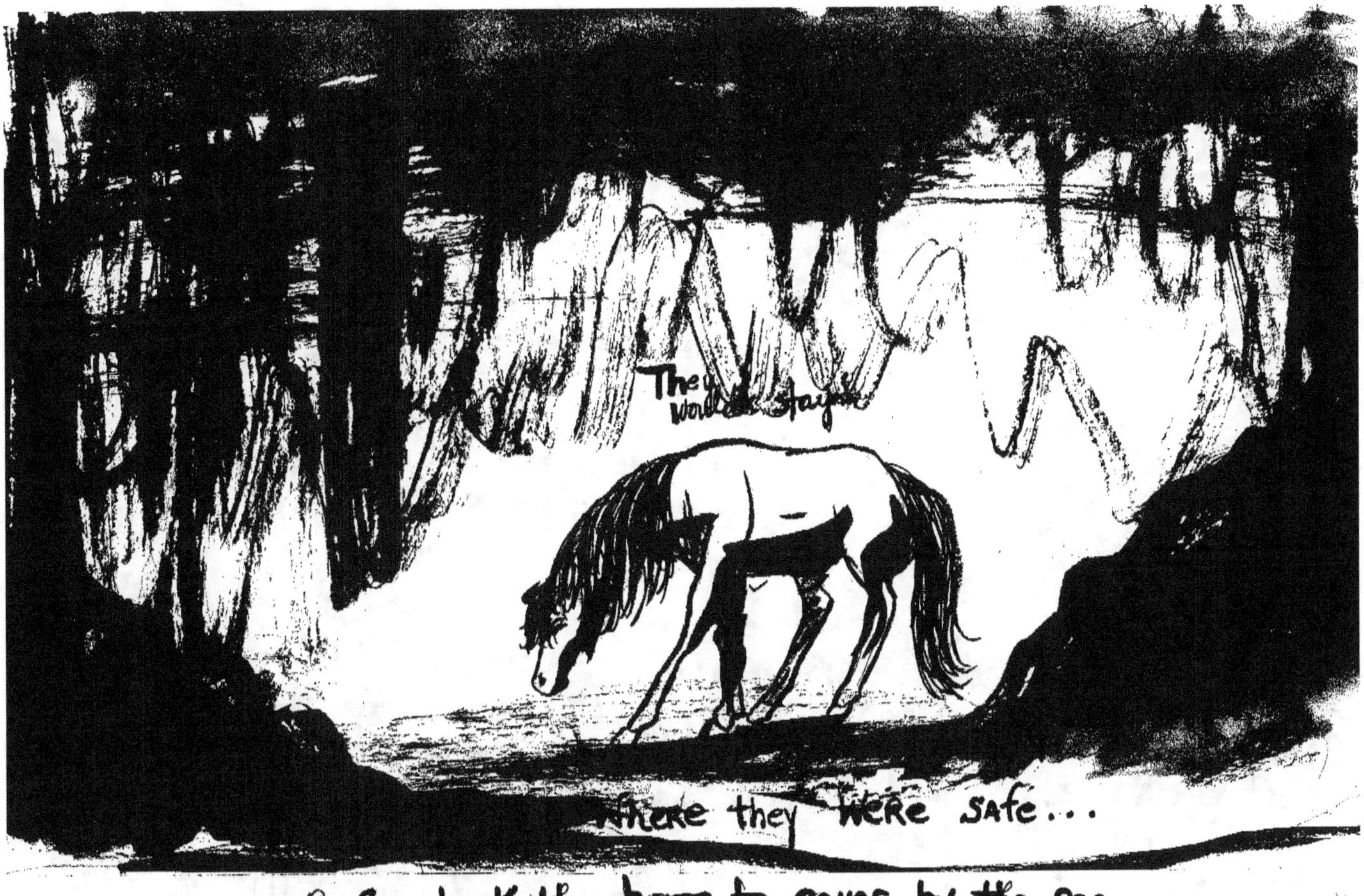

They would stay...

where they were safe...

The Boy took the horse to caves by the sea....

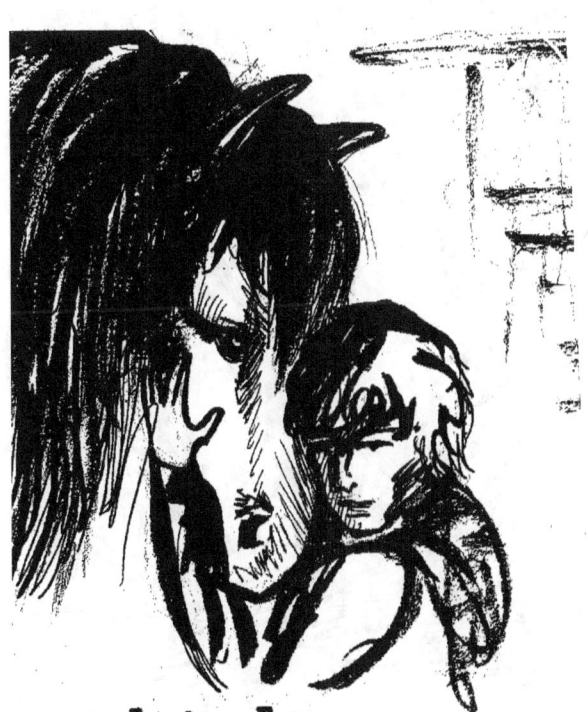

And friendship grew...

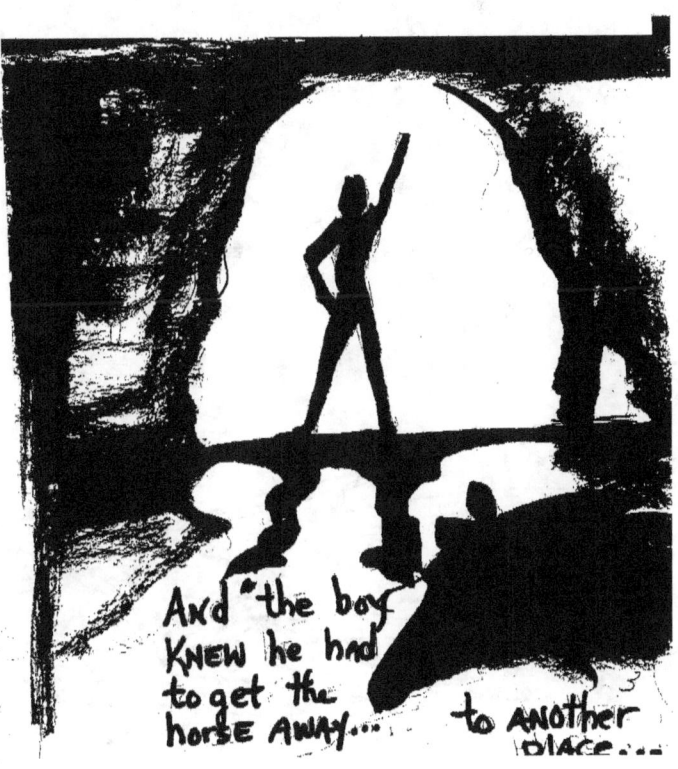

And "the boy KNEW he had to get the horse AWAY... to ANOTHER place...

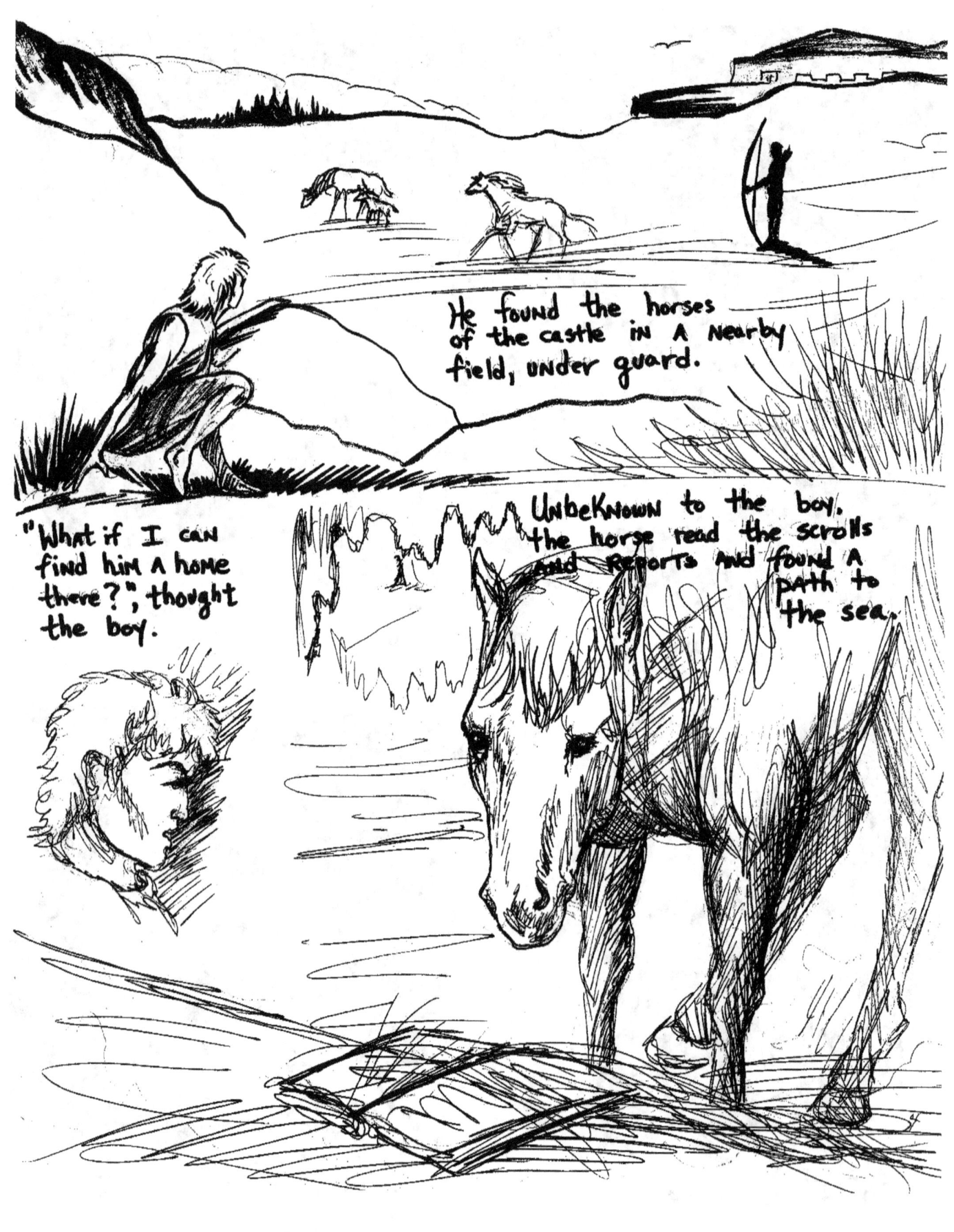

He found the horses of the castle in a nearby field, under guard.

"What if I can find him a home there?", thought the boy.

Unbeknown to the boy, the horse read the scrolls and reports and found a path to the sea.

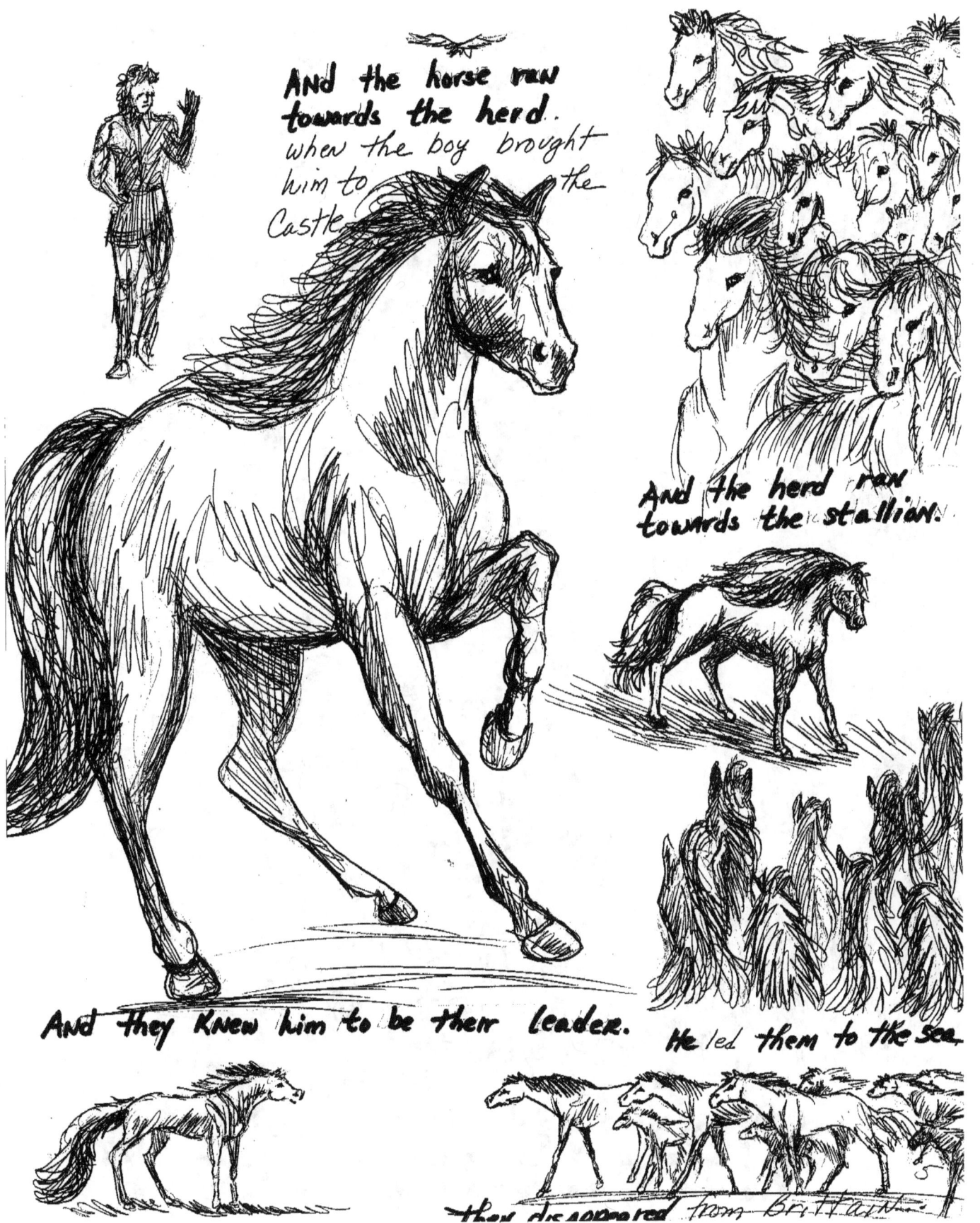

And the horse ran towards the herd. when the boy brought him to the Castle

And the herd ran towards the stallian.

And they knew him to be their leader.

He led them to the sea.

then disappered from Brittain.

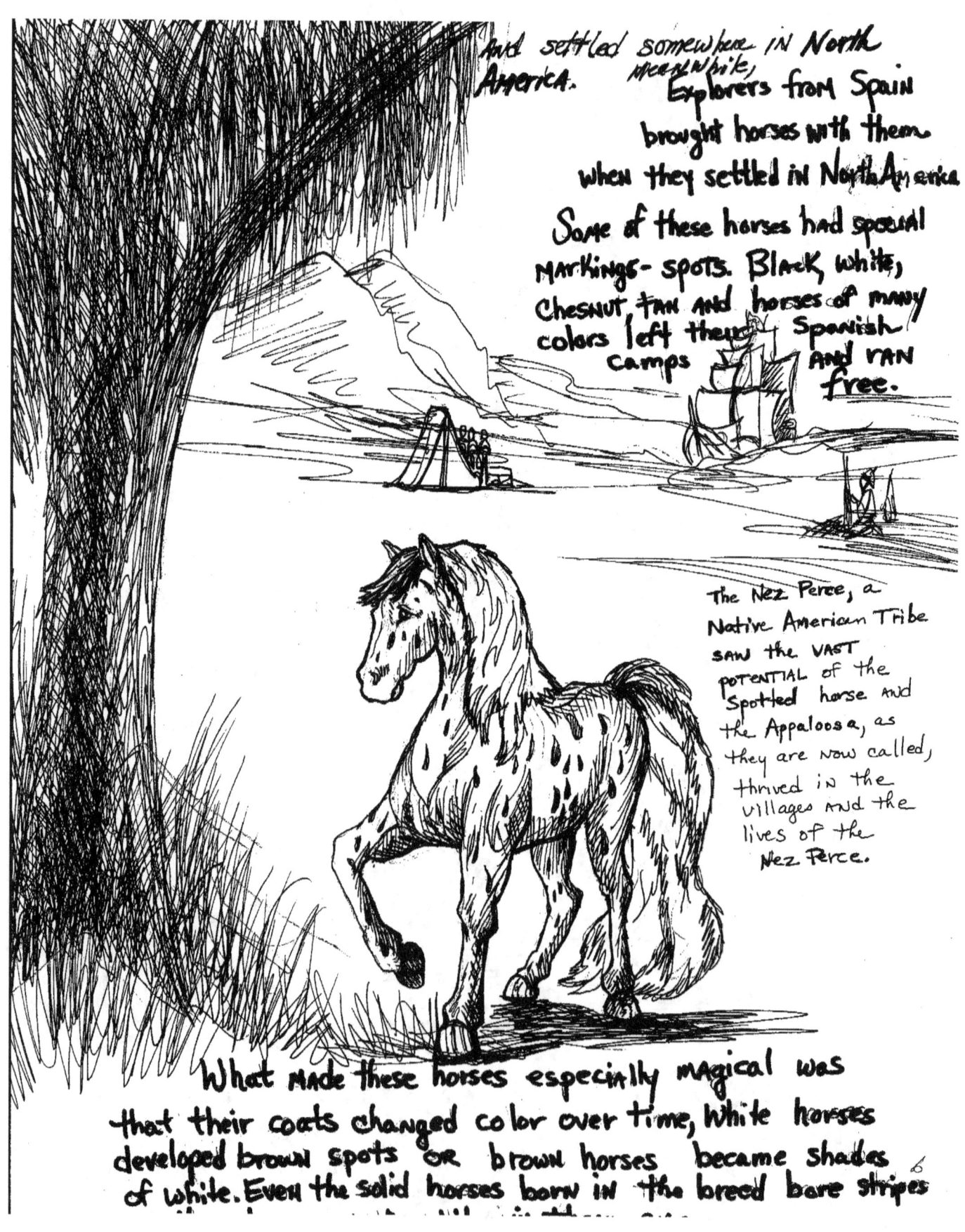

And settled somewhere in North America. Meanwhile, Explorers from Spain brought horses with them when they settled in North America

Some of these horses had special markings- spots. Black, white, Chesnut, tan and horses of many colors left their Spanish camps and ran free.

The Nez Perce, a Native American Tribe saw the VAST POTENTIAL of the Spotted horse and the Appaloosa, as they are now called, thrived in the villages and the lives of the Nez Perce.

What made these horses especially magical was that their coats changed color over time, White horses developed brown spots or brown horses became shades of white. Even the solid horses born in the breed bore stripes

There was a battle,...
Tradgedy struck and the spotted horses, called
Appaloosas, were separated from their families
and homes. Many died protecting their human friends
   Those who survived hid in the mountains.
Often alone, hungry and scared, the spotted
horses called to their ancestors, ancient Horses of long ago, for help.
The instinctive cry was heard miles away in
a cave by the sea. And the great horse of
Arthur came to the aid of the Appaloosas.

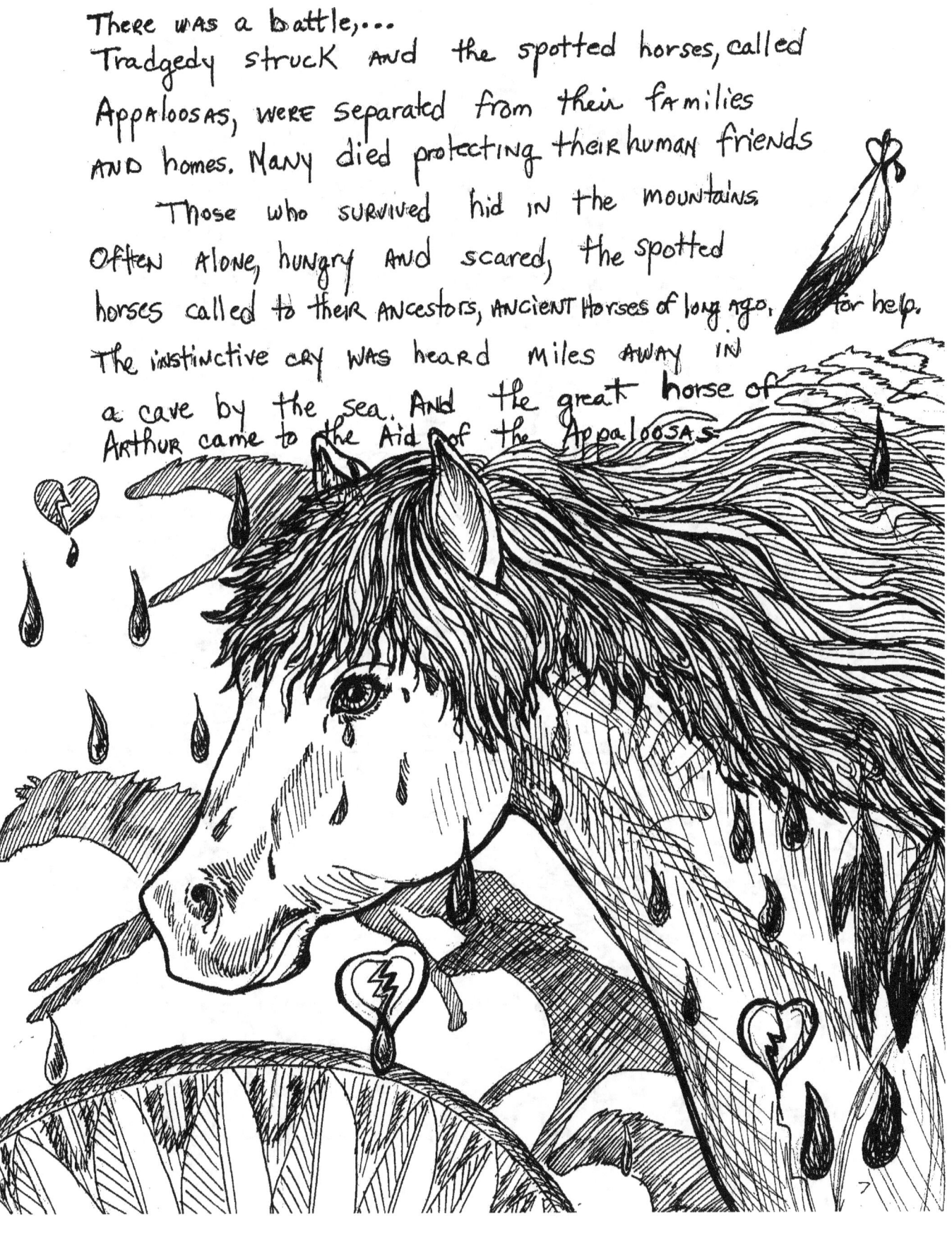

Winds carry change. Scattered, alone, the spotted horses roamed searching for one another. Taking care to avoid predators, they gathered in small bands, often without a leader. One particular young stallion sought the very hills where he grew up. He found them and settled there. One night he heard the wind call his name . . . and horses came out of the mist. Illuminated and warm the lead horse nuzzled him and joined the spotted stallion on his journey to gather all the remaining spotted horses.

Northwest United States

Apith the spotted stallion followed to gather his Appaloosa herd.

As if by magic, the spotted stallion could travel further, jump higher and hear more than any other horse. With his spirit horse guides, the spotted Appaloosa established a home for the herd, a place to be.

8

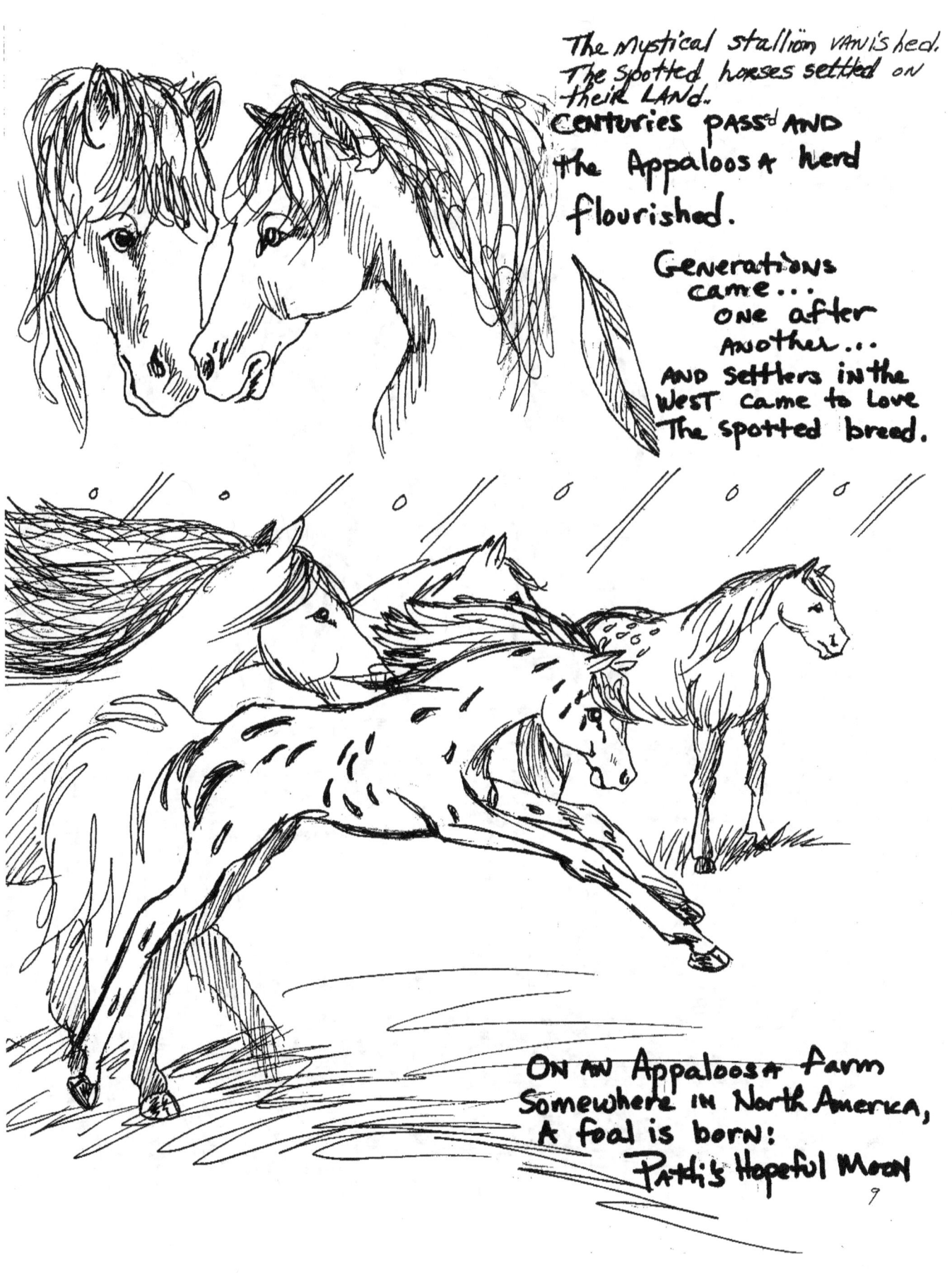

The mystical stallion vanished. The spotted horses settled on their land.

Centuries passed and the Appaloosa herd flourished.

Generations came...
one after another...
And settlers in the West came to love the spotted breed.

On an Appaloosa farm somewhere in North America, a foal is born:
Patti's Hopeful Moon

9

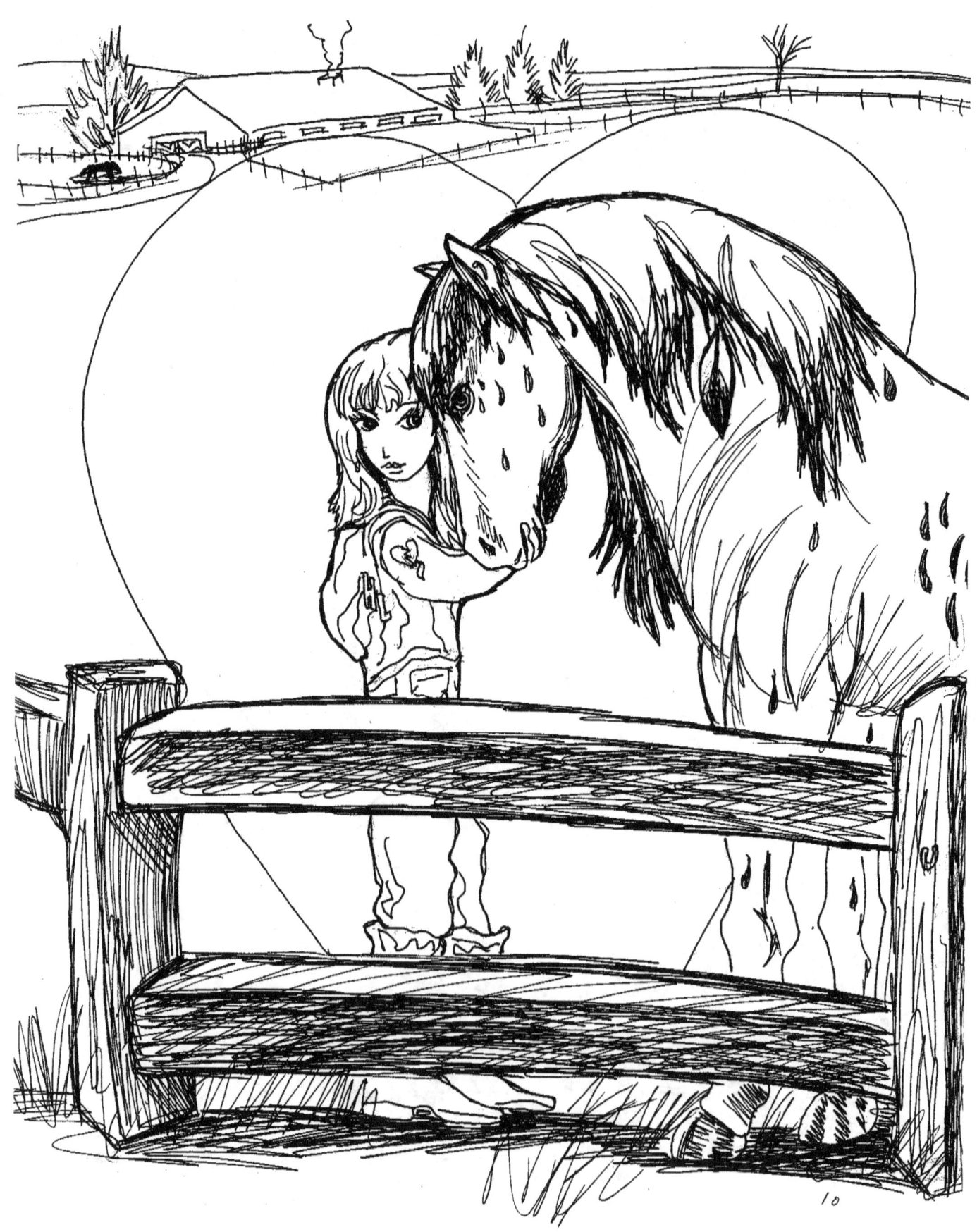

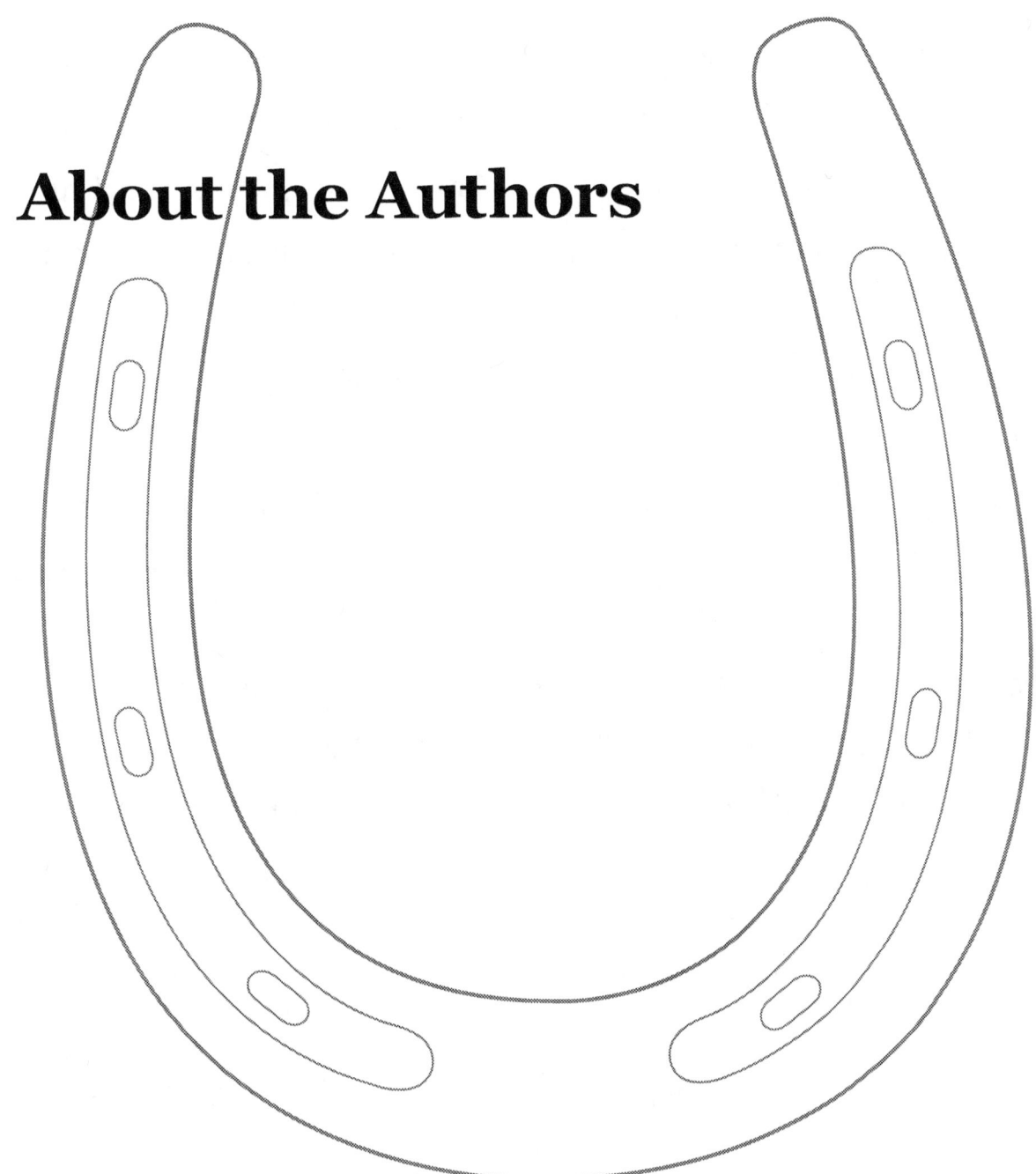

About the Authors

Dr. Maryann Pasda DiEdwardo and Patricia J. Pasda M.F.A. are a Master Teachers, Artists, and Authors. Current areas of expertise include graphic writing, painting, drawing, lectures on multi arts education as paradigm, environmental stability, distance learning elementary to graduate level, curriculum design and implementation, literacy, multicultural educational topics, educational psychology and instructional design theories, paradigms and models.

Bethlehem Area Public Library Art Exhibit and Demonstration for the
Public   April 1981-present

Lecturer, Storytelling, Art Demonstration, Exhibit Barnes and Noble
Booksellers and Borders Books Allentown and Easton PA
Public Exhibitions   October 2000-present

MODERN MUSIC TRANSFORMS THE COLLEGE ENGLISH CLASSROOM AND THE DISTANCE LEARNING VIRTUAL CLASSROOM SYNOPSIS

"Most importantly, music as a catalyst helps the student find a way to relate to the literary message and encode language through sound."

Maryann P. DiEdwardo

In 2004, statistical results of my case study research suggest that pairing music and linguistic intelligences in the college classroom improves students' grades and abilities to compose theses statements for research papers in courses that emphasize reading and writing skills (DiEdwardo 2004). In my initial study in 2003, I refined Howard Gardner's (1993) definition of music as a "separate intellectual competence" and compared music intelligence to linguistic intelligence. Furthermore, presently, in the enhanced or distance learning educational platform, I suggest that through acknowledgement of MI Theory, educators infuse cognitive abilities of students by helping them "think" as one of my students suggested. As Howard Gardner suggests, "Very worthwhile. The next step is to figure out why you got the effects that you did. Is music motivational? Does it activate other brain centers? Does it have some kind of intrinsic link to linguistic capacities? Would the effect work the other way around, or with other materials (2004 email)?"

Lectures and Demonstrations Lehigh Valley Community, Northeastern PA and Pocono Area for Businesses, Private and Public Schools, 1977-present. Modified list follows: Borders Books and Music Café, Barnes and Noble, St. Ann's Elementary School, St. Jane's Elementary School, Holy Family School, Asa Packer Public Elementary School, Farmersville School, Sacred Heart School in Bath, Sacred Heart School in Miller Heights, Our Lady of Perpetual Help School, St. Simon and Jude School, Holy Infancy School, Holy Family School, Notre Dame of Bethlehem, St. Michael's School, St. Elizabeth's School, Bethlehem Christian School, City of Bethlehem Historic District, Moravian Academy of Bethlehem, Bethlehem Area Public Library, Pocono Manor Lecture and Demonstration